Write A F*$%'ing Book Already!

The Insider's Guide To Increasing Your Sales & Improving Your Career With A Book

JIM F. KUKRAL

Published by Digital Book Launch

For book marketing help visit:

http://www.DigitalBookLaunch.com

Copyright © 2012 Jim F. Kukral

CONTENTS

BOOK ACKNOWLEDGEMENTS

To my wife Doreen who tirelessly edits and proofs my books and makes me look good, as an author, and in real life. You are an amazing woman who I love dearly. Thanks for all you do for me.

INTRODUCTION

The following has been reprinted with permission from the author. It was originally published in the Huffington Post.

For centuries, the author of a book has been a revered figure, a symbol of intellectual achievement, wisdom and wit, brilliance and, above all, prestige. Indeed, the book, whatever its contents, has been an item of iconic significance.

It's no wonder that a large percentage of people want to write a book. Some have motives that their composition in the covers of a book, however defined as a physical entity or a cyber-product, will make them rich and famous; some see such an achievement as an expression of their persona, their point of view, their record of a life lived, a work of the imagination and the fulfillment of a secret wish for immortality.

Some harbor hopes that they can establish careers as full-time writers in genre fiction, or self-help, or advice to improve the lives of others or on subjects that display their knowledge of cooking, history, politics, religion or whatever has absorbed their interest.

Whatever their motives, their ambition is an obsession and they are willing to take the time and muster the discipline to pursue their dreams of authordom, hoping that the words they compose will be read, contemplated and engaged with by others. It is, indeed, a noble aspiration.

Before the advent of the Internet and the e-book reader, publishing was dominated by a hierarchy of professionals who bought, judged, edited and distributed books through a process of middle men and a chain of brick-and-mortar outlets to sell their book offerings for a profit. For those who, for whatever reasons, were rejected by these professionals, there was always what has been called "vanity publishing," whereby the author pays for the production of his or her book that rarely, if ever, found its way into the distribution channel.

The divide between the professional publisher and the vanity author on the Internet has disappeared. The two are now on equal footing in the Internet distribution chain, which is surging and will eventually dominate the book business. Now, any author who writes whatever book he or she chooses is on equal distribution footing with the professional publisher on the Net.

The result, which I view as an unintended consequence, is that the floodgates have opened for the wannabe writer of book content and all those who hungered to write a book and see it distributed to a point where the self-published book will undoubtedly outpace the traditional book publishing industry by huge numbers, perhaps by millions.

Consider, too, the vast number of out of print books and the back list books of published authors that will be reincarnated on the net. Ten million available books on the net is not an unreasonable possibility.

It has spawned a huge new industry that covers every area of the book production and marketing chain. There are hundreds of outlets that can convert a manuscript into formats that will fit any platform. Apparently, any book content properly formatted is acceptable to the main e-book and POD retailers. Write a book and it can enter the system in days and theoretically compete with every other book in the marketplace.

Hundreds, perhaps thousands of book bloggers have emerged offering reviews, some paid for, presenting themselves as advertising mediums. Once respected and allegedly neutral industry review publications like *Kirkus* will review any book for a price that will undoubtedly offer some favorable quotes for marketing. Other such sites have sprung up as well.

Promoters of every ilk have emerged with the promise of getting one's book publicized and getting the author on TV and radio outlets. Social networking "experts" abound, promising to create author awareness on Facebook, Twitter and other open venues on the Net. Every form of promotion will have its "stores" on the net, many providing videos, apps, enhancements, and whatever else can be devised for a price. Determined authors with ample funds will be happy to part with their money in their attempt to realize their hopes and dreams.

Many sites offer free conversions and a distribution deal that takes a piece of sales revenue provided the author pursues his own individual marketing program, many of which are offered on the Net for a price.

Because of the vast volume of self-published authors who have been rejected by traditional publishers, it has become a numbers game, where the outlet who designs the content for sale in the online marketing chain takes a percentage of any sales generated by the author. The truth is that the vast majority of self-published authors will barely sell more than fifty to one hundred books, after his chain of friends and relatives have been exhausted. Thus, the company that produces the formats for distribution has found a way for the individual author to be a freelance sales agent for the company who has put the book into the marketing chain.

The company with the most books under contract can make a fairly hefty living with its battalions of authors out there beating the drum for their book sales. Small sales numbers for each self-published book adds up.

As for the quality of the book offering which, in any event, is subjective, the honest filters of the past will be rare. Anyone can be a self-proclaimed literary critic. Perhaps they will attract clusters of fans but there will be so many of them it will be difficult for a layman reader to make a choice.

The fact is that there is little chance for a self-published author to expect to earn enough to do such work full-time, unless he keeps his day job, has a pension, or is independently self-sufficient. Some might do it. Good for them.

I do not wish to cast any aspersions on the business practice of those who have discovered the benefits of catering to the self-published. It is legitimate and, in many ways, satisfies the hopes and dreams of the author who can now say he is a published author with his book in a respectable catalogue featuring books by other authors. A novelist can be in an online bookstore with the likes of Hemingway, Faulkner and Fitzgerald. A mystery writer can be in an online bookstore with P.D. James and Ruth Rendell. And so it goes for writers on any subject or genre.

This is not to say that there won't be breakout commercial books for self-published writers. The media will cover them, although some might be contrived or suspect. But even if legitimate, they will be few and far between.

I must confess that although I have been a pioneer in promoting the concept of e-books, I have been stunned by the vast explosion of self-published books. Perhaps this essay has stressed what some might consider the downside of the process.

Actually, the upside is far more gratifying. Writers whose voices had been silenced by the old system now have a chance to present their creative talents to a vast audience despite the difficulties of gaining traction in readership.

They can legitimately call themselves authors and be recognized as such, a satisfaction of great personal import. A press of a button will acknowledge that their work is out there for now and perhaps for all time for their descendants to acknowledge with pride. In some ways, they might consider themselves to have achieved some tiny piece of immortality.

Note I offer no judgments on the quality of these ventures only on the virtue of intent and accomplishment. To separate the wheat from the chaff will pose a monumental problem for readers and many talented writers might disappear in the vastness. Who knows how this will play out over time.

Nevertheless, I take my hat off to anyone who can sustain the creative process and find the discipline to write a long form work of the imagination, or can stick with the enormous mental effort to write a book on any subject. In the end, after all the dreams of fame and fortune fade with time, it is the work itself that really counted.

Warren Adler is the author of 32 novels and short story collections published in numerous languages. Films adapted from his books include The War of the Roses, Random Hearts and the PBS trilogy The Sunset Gang. He is a pioneer in digital publishing. For more information visit Warren's website at WarrenAdler.com.

WELCOME

I'm not going to tread lightly. In fact, I'm going to be very terse with you. The reason you grabbed a copy of this book is that you already know, deep down in your heart, you need to write a book if you want to take your career or business to the next level.

You've seen your competitors do it, yet you still don't take action. You've lost jobs because someone else branded themselves and built more credibility than you, yet you still don't take action.

Here's the tough love. Write a F'ing book already!

This book is meant to convince you that you must have a book if you want to win. You like winning, right?

Look, you need to make this happen. Not later. Now. This book is going to help you get it done.

In Part 1, I'm going to discuss why you must have a book and talk about what that book can do to help you win. In Part 2, I'm going to show you how other people, just like you, have done it so you can see how it's done and how it's directly affected their career or business. In Part 3, I'm going to give you tips and strategies on how to publish your book and use it to close more sales and leads, and create publicity.

Then it's up to you. So are you ready? It's time to write the F'ing book!

PART I – WHY YOU NEED A BOOK

CAN YOU SELL YOURSELF?

One thing you have to be really good at when you own your own small business, or when you apply for a job, is that you MUST be able to sell. Whether yourself or your business, it doesn't matter. You have to be able to close the deal.

If you can't sell, you're in a big trouble. Because the gal coming in right behind you probably can and, well, you're screwed.

Over my career I've sat on thousands of sales calls for myself or my clients. I've listened to masterful sales people create their spin and close business. I've made cold calls to potential clients and got to the point where I could tell if a customer is going to buy from me in 30-seconds or less.

I can sell you, if I want to. I'm good at it. I got you to read this book, didn't I?

I've also sat-in on hundreds of job interviews and watched as candidate after candidate came in, dropped down a standard, boring resume and completely flopped the interview, only to watch that person spend months, even years, trying to find a job because they simply had no idea how to sell themselves.

Yet, I haven't had a "real" job in over 10 years.

Sales is all about making sure the customer understands what you bring to the table that solves their problems, in the most appropriate way, based upon their specific needs and wants. To do that, you have to first understand what the customer wants, and why they are going to buy.

Then, and only then, can you effectively create a comprehensive message you can deliver to them that makes them say the magical words you've been dying to hear: "Yes!" or, "You're hired!"

Unfortunately, becoming a master sales person can take years and years to accomplish through practice and learning. And perhaps you don't really want to be a master sales person anyway (most don't). That's fine. There are ways to sell that don't require you to make thousands of sales calls or read 1,000 marketing and sales books (like I have).

In fact, that's what this book is all about. Oh, the irony. It's a book about how to make sales with books! Yes, this book is going to show you how having a book can change your life in many wonderful ways. So let's get this thing started, because you've got to finish reading this so you can go and start writing your book.

YOUR BOOK IS YOUR BEST BUSINESS CARD, OR RESUME

Bottom line: There is probably no better way to close a sale or get hired for a job than to pull a book out of your briefcase and let the person across the table know you are the expert in the industry.

Imagine this scenario. You're applying for a job as a social media strategist at a big manufacturing company. You really need a job, as you've been searching for something for months now. You keep going from interview to interview, and keep getting rejection after rejection for whatever reason. Maybe they didn't think you had enough experience? Maybe they just thought you were boring? Whatever, it doesn't matter. You can't seem to close the deal and get the job.

Then one day you finally say to yourself, "You know, I should write a book on my niche and my industry." So you go out and write something, put it on Amazon and get a few print-on-demand copies made. Then you go on your next job interview and you try this tactic instead.

The person across the table from you asks you a question about how you would do something and, instead of just answering verbally, you reach into your bag and pull out a copy of your book and say, "Well, actually, I wrote about this in my book. Let me just answer this for you. Let me find the page."

Briefly look up and see at the faces of the people across the table from you and you'll see the look in their eyes: "Wow, this cat wrote a book on this. He/she is the real deal." (Because that's EXACTLY what will happen.)

Now tell me, with that money move, are you getting the job, or is the other guy without the book getting it? The answer is yes, you're getting the job, more often than not. Believe me, I've seen it done to me as an employer and, frankly, it works. It immediately elevated that person to the top of the list in my head.

Here's the theory you have to admit is true. If someone has the passion/drive/skill/knowledge to go out and write a book on a topic, then logically that person must be an expert in that topic. Therefore, that person becomes a higher-level candidate for that position.

The same goes for all service type businesses as well. I don't care if you're a plumber, a car salesperson or an exotic pet seller of iguanas. You need a book!

QUALITY VS QUANTITY

This book is purposely shorter than most because I can make my point without wasting your time with a hundred extra pages. Remember this: There's nothing worse than someone writing way more than you need. In fact, it's just a waste of your time. I can make my point as quickly as possible, and get you on your way to writing, and then selling, faster.

This book is also purposely short because I want to illustrate that a book does not have to be long for it to be good and effective. The number one question I get at my book marketing firm called <u>Digital Book Launch</u> is, "How long does my book have to be?" The answer is: it doesn't HAVE to be any length. It could be 10,000 words, or it could be 100,000 words.

For a frame of reference, the average fiction book today is probably around 75k-100k words. The average non-fiction business type book, like my book, *Attention! This Book Will Make You Money*, is about 75,000 words. That equals to about 250 or so pages in hardback cover.

But again, you're not writing a fiction novel about teenage vampires, and the length of your book will not matter in the eyes of the customer you're trying to sell to. It is my opinion that the future of non-fiction type of "how-to" or biz/marketing books is going to be between 10,000 – 30,000 words. I firmly believe that, with digital books (the future), people don't want to spend hours and hours reading that type of content on their e-reader device. Sure, that may be different for vampire and romance novels, but for professional "how-to" types of books? No way.

I get why I keep getting asked about the-quantity-of-words-for-a-book question. The publishing industry has been keeping us from becoming authors for hundreds of years based on the fear of things like I just mentioned.

They have told us that:

- We can't write books because we don't know how to format them
- We can't write books because we can't sell them… only they can
- We can't write books because they are the only ones in the world who can decide if the content you create should be readable by the masses

It's all wrong. You know it and I know it. But perhaps, until just now, you didn't realize or believe it was ok for you to think that way.

So yes, your book is your best business card. Too bad it won't fit into your back pocket. However, it will easily fit into your backpack or briefcase and, believe me, it will have a much better effect on your chances of closing the deal than a business card.

WHY YOU CAN'T WRITE A BOOK! OR SO YOU THINK

Now we need to talk about why you say you can't write a book. Because wow, so many of you don't think you can do it. As usual with my most recent books, I tend to ask questions live to my social media friends so I can get immediate, and very real, reactions to put directly here in the book.

About 10 minutes ago, I asked people on Facebook and Twitter this question:

"Why haven't you written a book yet? Be honest."

Here are there unedited responses, and my answers to their objections below each one.

Rebecca Quinn *"It's such a big project!"*

My answer: It can be Rebecca, but it doesn't have to be. The traditional publishing system (which is failing) wants us to believe it's too hard to do.

They have been telling us for hundreds of years that we can't do it because it's too big of a project. The truth is that it's really not that hard. If you know a lot about something, you can put that into book form in a simple Word document. No special formatting. No special editing. It's as simple as you want it to be. Unfortunately, they've got you believing it's not that way.

Paul W. Swansen *"Write about what?"*

My answer: Ahh, the classic "I don't know what to write about" objection. If you're going to write a non-fiction book, like a "how-to" book like this one, it's easier to come up with ideas. As I'm sure you've heard many times before, it's all about figuring out what you know a lot about, what you're good at and what you're passionate about. Then write about it. But what happens most of the time is that you are devaluing your skill and knowledge.

I've seen it a million times. You seem to think what you know a lot about, or what you're passionate about, is "not good enough." I'm here to tell you right now, **it is good enough**. I guarantee that someone else in the world wants to know what you know, or wants you to teach them how to do what you do. Think about it.

Chris Cooper *"Not everyone has a story to tell?"*

My answer: I think you're wrong. Everyone has a story to tell. Everyone has something to say. You probably mean more like "I don't know what to say." Think about how you tell stories every day, about something you know a lot about or what you're good at. All you need to do is realize that you can take that knowledge and put it in book form.

Steve Kennedy *"Lack of focus…I am a polymath…much to my detriment at times!"*

My answer: I don't know what a polymath is, but it has the word "math" in it, therefore my brain just shut down. As for lack of focus, welcome to being just like everyone else in the world. I've always experience that focus is found when you can see the desired outcome that comes from the work involved. So I want you to try and envision a book cover with your name on it, or a book in your hand you can hand to a client or a recruiter. Or even better, a check that comes from Amazon with sales for your book.

William Ryan Harrell *"Before I wrote mine it always seemed a lot harder than it actually was. I always looked at it like this insurmountable task, maybe people are associating the old way of publishing to the new ways."*

My answer: That's right. After you write your first one, it's immensely easier to write the next ones. And you are right. Many people are looking at the old way of publishing and finding themselves intimidated. I'm doing my best to fix that in this book and others.

Jenn Ettorre *"Who would want to read what I have to say?"*

My answer: This is a classic response. Typical of people who simply believe what the publishing industry has been touting for years; that only important, famous writers can write books. Bullshit! Anyone can do this. You have stories to tell. You have things you know a lot about. You have passion. You can do it. It's time to start believing.

Eric Nagel *"I don't think I know anything (or have anything to say/write) that anyone would want to read. Plus, there are already so many outlets to publish content (podcast, blog, etc.)"*

My answer: I've pretty much covered the objections to "I don't have anything to write" already, but in terms of outlets to publish. Yes, there are many outlets to publish. But I want you to answer honestly. What has more credibility in certain situations like a job interview or a client pitch? A podcast you did, or a freaking book you wrote? A blog post you wrote, or a book you wrote? A video you made, or a book you wrote? You know the answer to that question.

Missy Tonkin *"I am working on it...there is just so much in my mind, and don't want to be redundant to other information out there!"*

Note: Missy is one of Disney's top travel agents. I'll give her a plug because she's awesome. Planning a trip to Disney? <u>Contact her</u>.

My answer: Worrying about redundancy is a trap. The truth is there are millions of books, blogs, videos and podcasts that all spout the same things over, and over, and over. Redundancy exists already, so why worry about it? Instead, worry about making your book better than the rest and using your skills as a marketer to make it help you with your agenda. Imagine a short digital book about "Missy's Top 25 Fantastic Disney Secrets For A Great Time" or something like that. It would be amazing! Redundant to the work other people put out, maybe… but who really cares if it works for your business?

Joe Sousa *"I get halfway finished with some of them but never get around to finishing the rest. Mostly because I think what I have written so far wouldn't be worth reading for most people."*

My answer: You gotta deliver, Joe! Maybe the reason you aren't finishing is because you're over-thinking them or trying to make them more than they really have to be? Again, stop devaluing yourself and your knowledge. (I think we need book therapy for people! Haha!)

Nick Throlson *"Borders went bankrupt & no one is buying books anymore!"*

My answer: So untrue, but nice try! For every 100 print books sold on Amazon, they sell 180 digital books. That's a direct quote from Amazon CEO Jeff Bezos. I can point you to numerous authors who are earning thousands of dollars per day selling books. Heck, I had my first $100 day in profits on my books the week before this. Oh, and that did not include my traditionally published book, just my own self-published books. You were right about the physical bookstores though.

Brett Bumeter *"I'm self-financing my way through mine. Ergo my business profits go into paying the bills for the time I take off to write, the money spent on marketing, (book covers have been tricky), editing, and audio production. Then again, I'm writing fiction not non-fiction."*

My answer: It might be time to read my book about how I pre-funded my book series by raising over $35,000 BEFORE I wrote the books? Check it out at <u>No Publisher Needed</u>. Problem solved!

JClevelandPayne *"Too many idea or pieces that I think are good enough to go into a book, but not enough time to really turn the ideas into one coherent theme. Also, too much in love with all of those idea to let go of a few to help the cause."*

My answer: Pick one and try to push out 10,000 words. Don't try anything else, just that. See what happens. I find that, once I start writing, a million other ideas come into place and what I had originally set out to write changes quite a bit. Writing is a process, not an exact science.

Jessica Baker *"Lack the discipline it takes to dedicate the time to focus on one thing! It always ends up de-prioritized."*

My answer: As I mentioned above. Perhaps you need to see the potential outcome and envision what you could get from it. Hopefully this book will help convince you.

PART II – THEY DID IT, WHY CAN'T YOU?

THEY DID IT, WHY CAN'T YOU?

One of the best tools that sales people use, to help make sales, is something called social proof. Social proof is the simple act of showing how other people have done something, or chosen something, therefore making you, the potential customer, feel more comfortable because other people have done it before you.

So, you realize it's my job to convince you to write a book, right? That's the entire point of this book. So naturally, I've got to include some social proof, right? Here you go. I've compiled a bunch of stories from real people who have used a book to change their lives, both personally and professionally.

MICHELLE COLLECTS MONEY... FROM HER BOOKS!

Michelle Dunn is an expert money collector. No, not the type that shows up at your house in a leather jacket with a bat in hand. You know, the professional-type of money collector. She specializes in helping businesses get paid by past-due clients. One of Michelle's biggest challenges, like most people, was finding new business.

So, Michelle decided to write a book. "I wrote my first book to promote my business. I owned a collection agency and my book title was *Starting a Collection Agency – How to make money collecting money*," said Michelle.

Michelle wrote the book and sent press releases to the local papers, business magazines and online media sources. Because of the topic and title, it got a lot of media attention. "As it turns out, there was only one other book anywhere about starting a collection agency. Once I did an interview with one newspaper, it snowballed to NPR and Ladies Home Journal, etc…".

"Writing this book gave my business much more credibility and, because of the media attention, more business," said Michelle. In fact, that book is now in its Third Edition. Michelle has since written 15 books and become so successful as an author that she sold her collection agency and is instead making a living selling her books online.

You can check out Michelle's Amazon page here.

NO FEAR IN THIS BUSINESSMAN, JUST PROFITS

Marc A. Pitman owns a business called FundraisingCoach.com where he helps organizations understand how to raise funds, of course! So, naturally, Marc wrote a book about it.

"My first book, *Ask Without Fear!*, was traditionally published through a small publisher in 2008," said Marc. "It's sold over 4000 copies in print and e-book format since then. While the sales are nice, the book has solidified my brand and significantly increased indirect income."

"Here are three examples. First, one firm was looking for nonprofit experts to develop an online site for fundraising training. They only considered experts with a certification and at least one book. I didn't have the certification, but I did have the book, so I was included. This is developing into a passive revenue stream."

"Next, a couple of event planners in Mexico were interested in putting on an event for nonprofits. When they Google'd "fundraising training," they found me. Because I had the book, and a professional looking site, they asked me to be the day's keynote."

"Finally, back when the JetBlue flight attendant jumped out of the plane to quit his job, I was asked to go on Good Day New York to talk about career change. The reason I was accepted on the show? My book on nonprofit fundraising. The producer talked with me, looked at the booked, looked at me, and approved. Although the book had nothing to do with career change, it gave me the credibility to be "legitimate.""

FASHION MODELS CAN WRITE? SURE THEY CAN

Amira Shiraz is a former fashion model turned entrepreneur who has created a successful speaking career and consultancy from her book. As Amira told me in an email interview…

"I am a personal branding strategist and coach with a recently published book, _Being Me: A Guide To Branding Myself Everyday_. I'm a believer that if people "brand" themselves using the same philosophies that companies use to brand their products, they will achieve their goals in life, both personally and professionally.

"Traditionally, while most people write books to become "bestsellers", that wasn't my priority. Publishing a book on a topic within my field has given me instant credibility and more doors have open for me business-wise. Before my book, I rarely booked speaking engagements. Since my release last fall, universities, school groups and organizations constantly reach out to book me for events, in addition to opening another revenue stream for my business for consultations."

SELL, SPEAK, PROFIT

David C. Baker writes books and uses them to sell from the back of the room (a practice where a speaker sells books to the audience after the presentation). His book, *Managing Right For the First Time*, is a intended as a field guide for first time managers, or for managers who want to do a better job.

I asked David how he uses his book to make money and boost his speaking career.

"I had a three-day conference last week and we sold $1,600 from a table in the back, at full retail," said David. "I'm speaking at Harvard in two weeks and will be giving away about 100 to students. In other words, they will be leaving the graduate program and immediately managing people. I'm hoping the book helps them… so that they'll also buy copies for other people who are promoted."

David has seen his books increase his consulting business as well.

GROW RICH FROM YOUR BOOK

Pete Peterson made about $81,000 a year selling his book in the back of the room at speaking events. Nice!

"In the mid-eighties I taught Think and Grow Rich in venues large and small. I was quite successful," said Pete. "To increase my income through 'back of the room sales', I wrote a specific-skills sales book, *Selling With a Purpose*, published by Franklin Hill Press.

"This increased my income substantially. I moved into "small city marketing," on the theory I'd have less competition since most motivational speakers would rather speak in San Francisco, New York or San Diego than travel to Omaha, Oklahoma City or Hannibal, Missouri. The next nine years proved this theory. I became a big fish in small ponds, speaking on sales as epitomized by *Think and Grow Rich*. I sent kids to college, bought houses, cars and clothes and travelled the world over. Since then, I have written other "with-a-purpose" books. Today I'm retired from speaking engagements, but I continue to write and coach a select few high achievers."

THE WOW FACTOR

Wayne English knows that being an author impresses people. "When I lecture on writing for the Web or social networking, that fact that I'm a published author, and that my next book is on social networking, is meaningful," said Wayne. "People know I'm serious, that I've done the work, and that it's good work. They listen to what I have to say. They read my blog."

Wayne has also used his book to get a new job. "Here was one specific instance where the book was instrumental in obtaining a technical writing job. I was speaking to the client when he asked for my resume, so it could be submitted to purchasing, as they needed to approve the contract. I told him that I was an easy-sell because my book was a Top 5 Business Title in Leadership books at The Washington Post. He said, "Wow," … and I got the job."

A GUIDE TO SUCCESS… FROM HER BOOK

Victoria Westcott recruits Canadian and American teachers to work in London, England, through her company, Classroom Canada. Naturally, Victoria realized that she should have a book that would attract new clients.

"I wrote the e-book, _Guide to Teaching in London: A Survival Guide for Canadians_ and I sell the book online for $29.95," said Victoria. "The e-book explains everything a teacher needs to know before making the move to work in London, so it's obviously a help in getting teachers that might not otherwise hear about Classroom Canada. The book also opens doors for me to offer workshops and webinars. Most recently, I was brought to McGill University to hold a 4-hour workshop on teaching overseas."

Victoria goes on to say that while she doesn't make a ton of money directly from the sales of the book she does, in fact, see an increase in business because of it.

GARDENING BOOKS CAN'T BE SUCCESSFUL

Can a gardener write a book and make money from it? Heck yes! <u>Colleen Plimpton</u> is the author of *Mentors in the Garden of Life*. She calls herself a "garden communicator" whose business, Morning Glory Gardens, was helped enormously by the print-on-demand (POD) publication of her book.

"My book gives huge credibility to my garden speaking business. When, in the course of delivering The Bins and Outs of Composting, or Not Tonight, Deer!, or Gardening is for the Birds, I hold up my book and announce its award. The audience actually applauds!," says Colleen. "I sell books at the back of the lecture room, yes, but I also get booked more frequently as a lecturer. I'm now seen as an expert."

"The book has also assisted me in snagging freelance work. I just signed a bigger contract with a regional Hearst division, for example, and I know one of the factors that singles me out from all the other garden speakers is my book. Another way the book has helped is when I announce, in my monthly gardening e-newsletter, that my garden is open for visitors on certain days. People come in droves. They want to see the gardens and plants mentioned in the book and, while they're there, they sign up for garden coaching, or ask me about lecturing to their group, or purchase plants."

MAKING THE BIG GUNS TAKE NOTICE

Jessica Setnick self-published a book entitled *The Eating Disorders Clinical Pocket Guide* to

help position herself as an expert in the eating disorders field. And boy did it work for her!

"After selling several thousand copies (including a large bulk order to be used as promotional gifts), I was recruited by the American Dietetic Association to write their eating disorders pocket guide," said Jessica. "Apparently the librarians at the American Dietetic Association were using my book as a reference when dietitians called in with questions about eating disorders. So when something came up in the publishing department about publishing a book on eating disorders, the librarians said something along the lines of "ADA should do something like this."

"I was contacted by an editor who asked if I would revise and update the book for a second edition, published by ADA. But things had changed so much since the first edition that I ended up writing a whole new book."

Jessica is now working with the American Dietetic Association to publish another book as well.

A PERSONAL STORY OF A JEW IN JAIL

Ever hear of the *Jew in Jail*? Me neither. But what a neat story. Gary Goldstein spent nearly six years incarcerated in various New York state prisons. During that time he wrote a book!

"I wrote my book as I was doing my time, with full confidence and knowledge that, while the public is always interested in prison books, they would be even more captivated to learn what it was like for a Jewish man – an alcoholic, drug addict and compulsive gambler – to do time as a minority behind bars," said Gary.

"Readers, listeners and viewers would likely find it fascinating to learn what my days and nights consisted of, as far as dealing with extreme prejudice and anti-Semitism, as a minority in prison, how I spent my time and dealt with the demons associated with my addictions, my ultimate recovery, and what the correctional system in the state of New York itself was like."

Gary is now a recovering addict who's graduated from an outpatient drug treatment program, and is the chairman of the alumni committee. He speaks to the current clients there, at detoxes and in schools. He recently completed a three-day motivational and inspirational speaking tour of Rikers Island.

SELLING JEWELRY FROM A BOOK?

Rebeca Mojica sells jewelry supplies. So naturally, she wrote a book about it! The book was instructional and showed folks how to make jewelry.

"Writing the book has brought us new customers and has increased our top line," said Rebeca. "The book helps us get new clients because my company, Blue Buddha Boutique, makes kits for every project in the book. If you "peek inside" the book or "download the free pattern" on Amazon.com you'll see a variety of finished jewelry pieces as well as individual components and tools. Blue Buddha sells all of these parts, so essentially the entire book is product placement for what we sell."

"The book has wide distribution, so it reaches people who otherwise would not have found us. We receive weekly calls and emails from new customers who've discovered us because they picked up the book at a local craft shop or bookstore, and now they'd like to try some of the projects from the book."

What a great idea! Imagine using your book to drive sales of your ecommerce store.

TWINS WITH LEARNING DISABILITIES DID IT, YOU CAN'T?

Identical twin sisters Brianna and Brittany Winner were born 11 weeks premature and spent the early years of their lives in-and-out of hospitals. At an early age, they faced the harsh reality of dyslexia. They fell in love with science fiction books and super hero comics. To escape exhaustion and struggles at school, they began to create worlds, characters and adventures.

In fourth grade, their learning disabilities began to take a toll on their self-confidence and self-esteem. They defined themselves by their disabilities and limitations rather than their abilities. Their father stepped in and reassured them they were talented, intelligent, and extremely capable. He recognized their story telling abilities and told them that, if they focused on their strengths and their passion for storytelling, they could do the impossible... write a novel.

They combined their love of comic books, adventure stories, and science fiction and, with the help of their father, began writing a book. They finished their first novel at 12-years-old.

The novel, *The Strand Prophecy*, won numerous awards including Best Adolescent Fiction, making them the youngest multiple award winning authors in America. At 13-years-old, their book was distributed nationally in all Barnes & Nobles stores. The twins regularly attended book signings, book fairs, comic cons as celebrity signers and industry trade shows.

At 14-years-old the Winner twins opened a nonprofit company, Motivate 2 Learn. Through their tour entitled "If You Can Dream It… You Can Write It!" they have spoken to over 100,000 students. They inspire students to read, write and overcome any obstacles they may face in order to achieve their dreams.

THE BOOK TURNED IT ALL AROUND

John Salat picks up business directly because of his book. Here's one of his stories. Why can't you do this?

"I dropped off a business card after a short interview and did not hear from them for months," said John. "After 3 months went by, I dropped off my newly released book. They followed-up with a call and asked me to start consulting there permanently. This is repeat work so the book, in a way, has created a steady stream of income."

"The other clinic approached me before I approached them. They saw my web site and, noticing my book, they took me seriously. I now work there permanently with a secure job. Both clinics also keep my book on file at the library, and patients sometimes buy books from me directly, allowing me to earn supplemental income."

IT AIN'T EASY GETTING OPRAH TO NOTICE YOU

Gabe Berman used his book to get noticed by guru Deepok Chopra, and possibly by Oprah!

"I wrote a book, *Live Like A Fruit Fly*, to prove that I could get published and then help change the world," said Gabe. "Like clockwork, however, I was rejected by every agent and publisher. Twice. So, I self-published through Createspace.com. From there, HCI, the original publishers of *Chicken Soup for the Soul* found my book and published it. Since, I've been endorsed by Deepak Chopra and I'm helping to help the world.

"The book is doing decently-well so far; about to be big. The last domino is about to tip. Through connections I made, through Facebook (believe it or not), the book made it to Oprah's Chief of Staff and I'm waiting on that."

25-YEARS OF BOOKS MAKING HER MONEY

Dr. Marlene Caroselli is an author, keynote speaker and corporate trainer. She has published over 60 books including *Hiring and Firing*, *The Critical Thinking Tool Kit* and *Principled Persuasion* (named a Director's Choice by Doubleday Book Club).

Her book tip? "When submitting a proposal, include the book. Very few things are more impressive, and more indicative of your qualification as an expert, than an actual publication."

Here's the story of how she did it.

"I was teaching part-time at National University in Los Angeles," said Dr. Caroselli. "I thought it would look more professional if I could hand out small books rather than stapled copies of the curriculum. So, very inexpensively, I had my book *PowerWriting* printed by Bookmasters in Ohio. The students (mostly working adults at Fortune 100 aerospace firms) were delighted – with the curriculum and the teaching that accompanied it – and began to tell their managers about the course."

"Soon, I was getting RFP-requests from these companies and from federal agencies. When I submitted my proposals, I included a copy of the book as evidence of my qualifications for teaching these seminars. The cost was minimal and I built it into my proposed fee for teaching the classes. The practice kept me in business for a quarter of a century, until my recent retirement."

PUT ANOTHER BOOK ON THE BARBIE

Cynthia Clampitt has used her book, *Waltzing Australia*, to explode her speaking business and gain publicity like she has never had before.

"My award-winning book, *Waltzing Australia*, has had modest success on its own," said Cynthia. "It has led to a lot of new writing opportunities but, more than that, it has helped my speaking career almost explode. I've gone from a few speaking engagements a year to one or two (paid) speaking engagements every week."

"Of course, one success helps the other, and more books are now selling — especially since the book was released in Kindle format two months ago. Still, even though I'm seeing more book sales, the speaking engagements far outweigh royalties as an income stream."

KAREN IS NO DUMMY

Karen Fredricks has used her books to become an instant authority in her field.

"I've written 13 books, 11 *For Dummies* books and two "cookbooks" (technology books), and created training videos for Lynda.com," said Karen. "The royalties have been nice, but being able to leverage the books into a successful consulting career has been even nicer."

How does she do it exactly?

"All the books include my e-mail address and contact information. I have links back to my website which provides me with a nice stream of prospects. When I come up against competition, or make a sales call to a large prospect, I plop down a copy of my book and tell them they can go with a lesser known competitor or with me, the expert."

PART III – TIPS ON GETTING STARTED

THE MANY DIFFERENT WAYS TO MAKE MONEY FROM YOUR BOOK

The point of writing a book is to use it to help you grow your career or make money, directly or indirectly. Writing a book is a lot of hard work and, as I've talked about in this book, you can use *your* book to help you get more sales, leads and publicity.

There are a bunch of different ways to do this. Not every strategy is right for everyone. You will need to decide which one is right for your agenda.

DIRECT SALES

You want the truth? Of course you do. The truth is that it's really hard to earn significant, life-changing income from the direct sale of a book. Even with the opportunity to earn 70% (what Amazon currently offers) commission from each book sold, you would still have to sell a lot of books, every month, to earn well.

I define "significant" income as $500 or more a month. That's money that you can use to pay a lot of bills. Add it up over 12 months and that's an additional $6,000 a year to your bottom line. Not bad. That's a really nice trip to Disney for your family or, for some, your rent paid for the year.

But to sell $500 worth of books, with a 70% commission, you need to sell a lot of books. Let's just say that you price your book at $5.00. Amazon is going to keep 30% of that ($1.50), leaving you with $3.50 in commission for each book. That means you need to sell 143 books every month to reach that $500.

Not as easy to do as it looks. The average author sells about 300-500 books for the LIFETIME of their book. Not a month. The LIFETIME of their book. Reason being, most authors don't really understand how important marketing is to book sales. The other reason being is that, perhaps, they didn't write a very good book, their cover is awful, or it was full of typos.

My point is that only a few authors really make a living from the direct sale of their books. If you happen to be one of those authors, then good for you. But most of us will use our books to make money indirectly from book sales. Here are the ways that can happen.

SPEAKING

Ever seem to notice that the speakers you watch, presenting on stage, always seem to have a book? There's no doubt that having a book helps event planners decide to select you as a speaker. As a matter of fact, I've spoken to many event planners, from small events to mega, super-sized events, and they have all told me that they tend to choose authors for their events, more often than not.

Patrick Snow, author of *Creating Your Own Destiny – How To Get Exactly What You Want Out Of Life & Work*, told me that he uses his books to help him stay on the road the majority of the year. "Whenever I have the opportunity to speak at an event, I always make sure to send a signed copy of my book to the event coordinator," said Mr. Snow. "More often than not, I get chosen because they are able to feel my book in their hands, and it helps them get a better feel for how credible I am."

Speaking at events can be a lucrative business. Authors with speaking careers can earn millions per year on stage. How would you like to get up to $10,000 or more for an hour of your time? Imagine jet setting around the world, speaking to people and getting paid for it?

A book can help you do that. At first, you're not going to command a $10,000 speaking fee. However, over time, as you build your credibility and fame, you and your book can move up in the ranks. Some events will even purchase copies of your book for their audience.

Tip: If an event cannot pay your required speaking fee, try negotiating that they buy copies of your book instead.

"BACK OF THE ROOM" BOOK SALES

One of the best things you can do when you are speaking is selling stuff in the back of the room. One of those things can be your book. Imagine this. You're on stage and you're about to wrap up your talk. You can easily mention that you will be making your way into the back of the room as soon as you get off stage, to sign copies of your book. Of course, they have to buy one and wait in line to get it.

Tip: Buy your print on demand books at cost from Createspace. As previously mentioned, depending on the length of the book, it will cost you on average $2.00 to $4.00 per book. That means you can upsell them for whatever you want and make big money.

Either ship the books directly to the event, or ship them to yourself first, and pre-sign a few boxes ahead of time. Ask your event planner to put them on display and assign a person to sell them for $20.00 a copy. If they balk at that, tell them you will split the profit with them. It's not uncommon to see a professional speaker carrying around stacks of books to sell and shipping them from city-to-city.

Another great tip is to give away a few copies of your book during your talk. Keep referring to the book during your talk, and ask questions to the audience by saying, "The person with the correct answer wins a copy of my book". Hold up the book, and then hand it to the person right from the stage. This will make sure they are aware of your book, and make them want to have a copy. Oh yeah, kick some butt on stage, or nobody is going to want your book.

CONSULTING

Professionals realize that a book adds credibility. Personally, my books help me close business on a daily basis. I would guess that 95% of my consulting clients start with this sentence when contacting me. Client: "I just finished reading your book and it was amazing. I just had to contact you."

This is exactly why I put a call-to-action, with how to contact me, in the back of every single book I write. Books create opportunities, period. The key to getting consulting gigs from your book is to make sure you write a book for your specific target audience. Let me give you an example.

I have a book that entitled, _Internet Marketing for Business Answers_. It's a wonderful book, filled with interviews from over 17 of the Web's most successful Internet Marketing experts. The book covers all topics from search engine marketing, to affiliate marketing, to email marketing, to social media, and much more.

In other words, the book is written to answer questions and solve the problems of my potential customers. And, of course, who's going to be there to help them solve those problems after they read the book? Me.

Don't make the mistake of writing the book that _you_ want. Do that, someday, when you're rich and bored, and don't need the money or fame. Instead, you should write a book that your audience wants and needs. That way they flock to it and, then, to you.

Tip: Always have a strong call-to-action at the end of the book. What I have done successfully in one of my books is to offer a free, no-obligation, consultation with me. That's where my leads come from daily. Imagine that, a daily source of leads flowing directly into my inbox without having to spend a dime on advertising. There's no reason you can't do it too.

MEMBERSHIP SITES & INFORMATION PRODUCTS

If you aren't a consultant then you can sell other stuff too. With a book you are an expert, so people want to buy from you. They want to be helped by you. You just need to decide what business model you want to put in place to help them.

One of those things could be a membership website, or an information product. I'll give you an example of how I'm doing it.

I'm the owner of a book marketing company that offers book marketing services. So I need authors, as they are my target audience.

I have created a book marketing resource, Author Marketing Club, which helps authors figure out how to be more successful. As authors become members, I continue to provide free book marketing tools and resources. That won't ever change. However, at some point, I will also have a new paid membership level for authors who want to really take their success to the next level. Or, perhaps, I'll have an informational product that I can offer to them.

You do have an agenda, right? This is business. Making money is not evil. If you can provide high-quality value to people who need it, there is nothing wrong with charging for it. In fact, if you do it right, your customers will thank you for it.

Tip: Try the free model first. You don't always have to start out selling, selling, selling! Create a community, or download that is free, and use it to bring in a lot of potential customers. Get them inside a community or at least on an email list.

COURSES AND TRAINING

This is very similar to the membership site and information product plan just talked about above; however, with a different methodology. For some reason, there are a lot of people who will never, ever, join a membership program or download an information product.

Those people tend to respond well to courses and training modules for whatever reason. Create a 10-week boot camp, or a 3-day training course, that they can purchase. Some people simply respond well to this type of learning.

Tip: Always include a time length commitment with your training or course. Why? People are busy, and they want help fast. Nobody is going to sign up for the 12-month training course you're offering. That's a lot to commit to. However, they might just commit to a 5-day boot camp, or a 6-week training course.

SHOULD YOU SELF-PUBLISH OR GET A BOOK DEAL?

The big shift is happening. The industry has completely changed. No longer do you need an agent or a publisher (gatekeeper) to get a book published. Retail bookstores are on the way out, and digital books are on the rise. Jeff Bezos, CEO of Amazon, has said that for every 100 print books they sell, 180 digital books are sold. Imagine what that stat is going to be in a 1-, 2- or 3-years from now? Wow.

I could write an entire book about why you should self-publish rather than traditionally publish. However, right now I'm going to offer a few concise reasons that self-publishing is the way for you to go.

A BOOK IS A BOOK, PERIOD

There used to be a distinction between a digital book (or e-book) and a printed book, but not anymore. A book is a book, plain and simple. It doesn't matter how it's delivered.

However, I do understand that there are still plenty of folks out there who don't see it that way. Some people still drink the Kool-Aid that the traditional publishers have made us drink forever, making us think that only printed books by big publishers, sold in bookstores, are books.

Let me tell you something. I don't care how I deliver it, or what format it's in. It's a book if I say it's a book. If I put a cover on it and put my heart and soul into it, it's a book. If I choose to not upload it to Amazon and give it away on my site, it's still a book.

"The Matrix is control, Neo". This nonsense about how self-publishers aren't real authors, or don't really write real books, is all a made-up form of control from the industry that wants to keep their power.

You know why most people don't write books? I do. I talk to them every day. The #1 reason they tell me is that they don't believe they can do it. Why? Because they say, "If you want to write a book, you have to get an agent, and a book deal. You have to figure out how to format your book just right, and you have to have perfect grammar, and so on."

YOU'RE GOING TO DO ALL OF THE MARKETING ANYWAY

So why pay a publisher their cut? Unless you're a proven best seller you aren't going to get much marketing help from your publisher. So it doesn't make much sense, does it?

YOU CAN GET IT DONE FASTER YOURSELF

Traditional publishers can have a 9-12 month cycle to getting your book published. Who has that amount of time to wait? As an entrepreneur or executive looking for a job, are you willing to wait around for a year or more? I wouldn't recommend it.

BOOKSTORES? WHAT BOOKSTORES?

If you honestly believe that you'll be able to walk into a super-sized bookstore in two to three years from now, sit down, have a cup of coffee and browse books… well then, I have some swamp land to sell you in Florida.

Besides, bookstores are completely pointless to you, and the reason you're writing this book. Forget about bookstores. They are a waste of your time.

YOU KEEP THE RIGHTS

Why would you ever want to give the rights to your book to another company? That would be like giving your proprietary system to someone and giving them control over it. It's a bad business deal, no question about it.

When you give away your rights, you can do nothing. You can't price your book the way you want. You can't change the cover art. You can't sell it where you want. You can't do anything without the permission of the publisher. Why in the heck would you want to do that?

YOU'RE NOT GETTING A BOOK ADVANCE

Sorry, you're probably not. The book business as it existed is dying. Publishers are not walking around throwing money to people who have no previous book-selling experience. Sure, maybe if you're a celebrity or other well-known person, they might throw some money at you.

I'm sorry to say that Jersey Shore star Snooki has two books by a traditional publisher, for which she earned signing bonuses. If that doesn't tell you everything you need to know about the state of traditional publishing today, I don't know what will.

YOU CAN MAKE MORE MONEY

After your agent takes a cut, and then the publisher takes a cut, you're probably left with about 17.5% of the profits from each book sold. And that's only after the initial run of your books is sold-out or your signing bonus is reached (the earn-out, as it's called). In other words, you're not getting a dime until they sell enough of your books to make back their money.

If you self-publish, you can sell the book yourself through Amazon and other sources, and earn up to 70% per book. You can even sell the book yourself through your website if you want, and earn ALL of the profits. I'll talk some more later about print on demand and how to use that to sell your books as well.

Convinced yet? If you want to learn more about this argument just head on over to NoPublisherNeeded.com and get more reasons why you should self-publish. (Yes, that's my blog.)

JUST WRITE, BABY!

Don't worry about length and format and all that stuff. Just write. Open up a Word document, start writing and keep writing. Someone else can format it later, and someone else can edit and proof it later. Until you get it down and out of your head, it's nothing. Nada.

The thing that stops most people from finishing a book is worrying about all that other stuff. Just write, baby!

HOW DO I GET THE BOOK UPLOADED?

With Amazon Kindle Direct Publishing, you simply register for a free account and follow a few short and simple steps to putting your book up on Amazon. In fact, if you want to see how darn simple it is, just register for free at the Author Marketing Club and watch the video where I show you how to do it, step-by-step.

To summarize, you just need to have the following things in order before you start:

- Book title and subtitle
- Description of the book
- Book cover in digital form
- Book manuscript
- The price for your book

That's it. After you click "save and publish," your book will be live for the world to see on Amazon in 24-hours or less. And the beautiful part of it is, if you ever want to make changes, you simply log back in and edit whatever you wish.

I do this all the time with updates to books, new book covers I want to test or for changing the price to see how it sells at different levels.

JUST DO IT YOURSELF

You're going to run into plenty of companies that will offer you a "turnkey, easy way to upload your book" for a fee. I have nothing against these companies. Most of them provide good services that work. However, most of them also want to take a cut from your book sales for the effort.

In all honesty, you can easily do all of this yourself with a few tips and lessons. There's really no reason to pay a bunch of money to someone who wants to eat into your book profits forever for something you could do on your own in 30-minutes.

Not to mention, when you want to make changes to your book you have to go through them and that can take days, or even longer. I've found that it's best to have the control to do whatever you want, whenever you want, on your own. For example, you may wish to test out a new price point on your book, or upload a new cover, or change your description, or add new categories, or a million other things you can do to test your book sales and ranking.

Why give up that control to someone else? The business of selling books in today's digital world is all about moving fast and adapting to the marketplace and the readers that support it. Just do it yourself. It's not that hard. Stop by the Author Marketing Club for some free videos and tutorials on how to get it done.

WHAT ABOUT PRINTED BOOKS?

You can, and should, still produce printed books. Nowadays, you can do this very easily using print-on-demand services, or POD. For every book I upload digitally, I also and create a POD version which allows my readers to order the book in print format, if they wish.

Yes, it is way more impressive if you walk into a potential client's office with a printed version of your book. I get that, and I believe it. That's why POD is so great. Companies like Createspace offer you the ability to upload you book manuscript and cover art, and they'll make your book available to purchase one-at-a-time, in print format.

The great thing about this is that they can also link directly into your Amazon page where you can offer the digital version, and the print version. When someone orders a print copy through Amazon, the order gets sent to the POD company and they print one copy of the book and mail it.

The reader has no idea that there's not a warehouse with 10,000 books waiting to be ordered and, frankly, they don't care. They just know they're getting a print copy sent to them.

The other great thing about POD is that it's very inexpensive to buy your own books at cost. For a 100-page book, you can probably buy a single copy from them for around $2.00 each. Then you can order boxes of them to keep on you and carry around to your speaking gigs, or to give to clients.

Heck, you could even sell them on your website, or in the back of the room at an event, for $10 or $20 each and make huge profits. The point is, for a few bucks, you now have a wonderful business card that will help you achieve your goals.

DIGITAL BOOK LAUNCH FORMULA

I've self-published six books at the time of this writing, with plenty more to come. Through my experiences doing so, I've developed a tried-and-true system for how to make a successful book marketing campaign… one that actually helps you sell books!

It is my opinion that book marketing should start at book conception. The very moment you have the idea for the book in your head, you should follow the formula I call "Concept, Cover, Convert".

CONCEPT

You've got the idea in your head. You've decided you should write a book about iguanas, because you are the world's leading expert on iguanas. Your customers are people who buy iguanas from you, so it makes sense to build your credibility, so they trust you more and only want to buy from you, and you alone.

You come up with a great title, *Everything You Always Wanted to Know About Iguanas*, and you write a short book summary about the book and what they will learn when they read the book.

That's it. You're done with Concept. You can now move onto the next step, Cover.

COVER

Can you guess what element of a book is the most important? Seventy-five percent of 300 booksellers identified the look and design of the book cover as the most important component. They agreed that the jacket is prime real estate for promoting a book. On average, a bookstore browser will spend eight seconds looking at the front cover and 15 seconds scanning the back cover.

So, as you can see, having a great book cover is extremely important.

A book isn't real until you put a cover on it. And if the book isn't real yet, it's just an idea floating around in your head, and maybe you'll never get to it. You need to have a cover made, immediately.

When you have a cover, you can better imagine the book. You can get excited, and motivated, to write because you know what it's going to look like. You can also begin to pre-market the book because you have something real to show potential readers.

Imagine going onto Facebook, or sending an email out to your customers, saying "I'm going to write a book". Big deal. Nobody is going to be impressed or get excited. However, if you include what the book cover is going to look like in that email, you're going to see a much different reaction. Why? Because it's more real… to you and to them.

And because it's more real, you have a much better chance of getting them to Convert, which is step 3.

CONVERT

The biggest mistake most authors make is they wait to market their book until after it's written. HUGE mistake. Convert is the most important step in the formula. Because convert is where you build awareness for your book, and also get people to give you their commitment to buying the book, later on when it's done.

Typically, this is done through a very simple landing page. The landing page is designed to do one thing… get them to show interest in the book. You are trying to get them to give you their email address, or/and like your book page on Facebook, or follow your Twitter account.

Remember, you haven't even written a word of the book yet, except the title and the description. With your new landing page you can begin to market the book instantly and build a database of people who want to buy your book down the road.

If it takes you 6-months to write your book, who cares? You can keep your followers up-to-date, all along the way, by sending them periodic notes and keeping them excited. Then, when your book is done, it's simply a matter of launching it to your newly built platform of readers and watching as your book sales skyrocket.

The alternative? Don't tell anyone you're writing a book. Wait until it's done and then, one day, go to social media and say, "Hey, I have a book out! Come buy it!" Sure, you'll make a few a sales, but nowhere near as many if you had used the methods above.

By the way, contact me to learn more about my book launch formula. (See that sneaky call-to-action?) Practice what you preach!

ADDITIONAL BOOK STRATEGIES (QUICK-HITTING TIPS)

You can buy your printed (POD) books at cost, and use them as giveaways on your site, or send them to prospective clients. Try this. When you close a deal, send a box of signed books, always. Include some candy or some cookies for a memorable treat.

Give away the books at speaking gigs, or sell them. You're only paying a few bucks for them anyway. Remember, it's your best business card.

Always carry a copy of your book around with you, wherever you go. You never know when you might need one to give away. I keep a box of them in the trunk of my car, always.

Forget bookstores. You're not getting in them. They're a waste of time. Don't even worry about bookstores, ever again.

HOW & WHY DID I PUT THESE STORIES IN THIS BOOK?

You may be wondering how I found so many wonderful stories to include in this book? I'm about to let you in on how I did it, and you won't believe how easy it was to do, and how it can help you write you own book as well… and fast.

First of all, let me explain the power of social proof. I've written about this in many of my other books as well, and talked a little bit about it earlier in this book. Social proof is when people get "helped" into making a decision, because they see other people who've done it. That's my unofficial explanation.

You know what I'm talking about. Testimonials are a great example. Reviews are a great example. Recommendations are a great example. When you see, or hear, that other people have done something, or bought something, or used something, (or whatever), you instantly give that concept a higher quality score in your head, which helps you make a decision.

You think, "Well, if they used it, and if the reviews are good, and if my buddy recommended it, then it must be good."

You know you do. ☺

As a marketing and sales person, this is probably the number one tool that I use in my toolbox; hence, all the great and powerful case studies I just showed you. Didn't those stories, from real people, motivate and empower you and help convince you to do it?

As I've always said to potential clients. "Look, I can talk ALL DAY about how good I am, and how I can help you, but you know what? Here are my customers. Call them directly and ask them about me. Here are my references."

Guess what? 90% of them never call. And guess what, again? It's the power of social proof.

So, when you write your book, consider going out and finding stories and case studies from other people to help you prove your point.

But you don't have to just focus on case studies. You can build a book from interviews as well. My book, *Internet Marketing for Business Answers*, is a book filled with my interviews with seventeen big-time Internet small business experts. I had search engine experts, social experts, affiliate marketing experts and more.

I conducted the interviews either by email or by phone. The phone conversations were recorded. Then I had them transcribed online, (for dirt cheap at Elance.com,) and put their interviews in the book. That's it! An instant book that I didn't even have to really write!

Ok, so how did I do this? How did I find the people to interview and all the stories? What's your secret, Jim?

One word: HARO.

HARO, otherwise known as HelpaReporter.com, is a free, Web-based service that connects sources with media. An easier explanation would be that it's a site connecting subject-matter experts (you and me) with journalists. For example, a reporter could be looking for experts who know a lot about the game of chess, so they send out a query on HARO asking people who know a lot about chess to contact them, and to possibly be included in their story.

It's a great idea, right? I've personally had stories in over 20 different media sources because of the direct contact I've made with journalists on HARO. I've also built some very nice relationships with those same journalists over time, allowing me to pitch stories to them from time-to-time.

Here's how it works. Go to HARO and sign-up as either a source or a reporter. On their website, they say this about reporters:

"Tap into the largest source repository in the world, with over 80,000 main street and expert sources, who will respond directly to your query on your terms. No more flipping through your rolodex, searching out-of-date databases, or being bothered by unsolicited sources with off-topic pitches. Submit your query and let HARO deliver the perfect sources right to your inbox."

They explain sources like this:

"From The New York Times, to ABC News, to HuffingtonPost.com and everyone in between, nearly 30,000 members of the media have quoted HARO sources in their stories. Everyone's an expert at something. Sharing your expertise may land you that big media opportunity you've been looking for."

Now you may be asking yourself, "Ok, but I'm not a journalist, so why do I need this site?"

Aha! There's the dirty little secret that not many people know. You do not have to be a reporter to submit a query. You don't need press credentials, or some special pass, or anything. You just register and make your pitch.

That's exactly what I did to get all of these stories in the book. I logged into HARO as a reporter and pitched this. See image below.

DETAILS	
Title	Author Success Stories Wanted
Query	Have you published a book that has helped your business or brand get more sales or leads? Have you published a book that has helped you get a job? Traditional published or self-published authors welcome. We want to hear your success for our new book, which is about how people write books to increase success. No, we're not talking about $$$ sales. More indirect sales. Example: you're a consultant who wrote a book to help you increase awareness and your brand.
Requirements	You must either be the author, or have access or permission to tell the author's story, with specific examples of success.
Media Outlet	Digital Book Launch
Visibility	Not Anonymous
My Deadline	2/5/2012 7:00:00 PM, EST
Targeting	Business and Finance --General ,
Status	Closed - No Longer Accepting Pitches
Query Email	query-1v7b@helpareporter.net
Submitted From	10.11.0.11

In a few days my query was sent out to over 102,000 "sources". That just means you and me. Subject-matter experts. A few minutes after the query was mailed, I began receiving emails from authors all over the world who wanted to tell their story for this book.

In total, I received about 150 emails from authors. I conducted email interviews with each one, took the best and put them in this book.

It's that simple.

I've just told you about two powerful ways to write a book in no time at all, without even really having to write!

CONCLUSION

YOUR FINAL MISSION

What else is there left to say, besides…

Write A F'ing Book Already!

As a matter of fact, I've got a recorded video training program that goes along with this book that you can subscribe to today. Just visit this link to enroll:

http://www.DigitalBookLaunch.com/writeabook

In this training you will learn how to write a book from start to finish.

Want a bonus? After you write your book, I'd love to give you free access to a book I wrote called *The Ultimate Digital Book Promotion Handbook – The Author's Guide To Finding Places To Promote Your Book Online.* Simply visit AuthorMarketingClub.com and sign up to get it.

A PLEA TO YOUR GENEROUS NATURE

If you've found this book helpful in any way, would you please consider going to Amazon and leaving a review? A big part of how I make a living is based off of how my books are shared and read online. Amazon reviews are a HUGE part of that. I would consider it a personal favor, and would be happy to reciprocate a favor to you, at any time. Just ask.

Sincerely,

Jim F. Kukral

ABOUT THE AUTHOR

Jim F. Kukral writes books that inspire and educate readers on how to improve their lives, careers and businesses. He is the CEO of a groundbreaking book marketing agency called Digital Book Launch. Contact Jim at **www.JimKukral.com** for a free consultation about your new book idea or existing book.

The following is a list of some of his most recent work. You can see a complete list of all of Jim's books by visiting **JimKukralBooks.com**.

Business Around A Lifestyle Volume 1 – How To Dream Your Perfect Lifestyle, Then Go Get It

The Ultimate Digital Book Promotion Handbook - The Author's Guide To Finding Places To Promote Your Book Online

Internet Marketing For Business Answers – Small Business Experts Edition

What Is Personal Branding? – How To Create A Memorable & Powerful Brand That Sells YOU!

No Publisher Needed – How I Raised Over $35,000 In 30-Days To Write My Book

How To Catch Happy – A Guide To Reeling In The Biggest Fish Of All

Attention! This Book Will Make You Money – How To Use Attention-Getting Online Marketing To Increase Your Revenue

www.ingramcontent.com/pod-product-compliance
Lightning Source LLC
Chambersburg PA
CBHW070121010626
45794CB00012B/1161